Raphael

DOORS

Sister Raphael SLG

SLG
Press

© 2023 SLG Press
First Edition 2023

Fairacres Publications No. 199

Print ISBN 978-0-7283-0346-1
Fairacres Publications Series ISSN 0307-1405

Edited and typeset in Palatino Linotype by Julia Craig-McFeely

Biblical quotations are taken from the New Revised Standard Version of the Bible unless otherwise noted in the text.

Pictures reproduced in this book were sourced through Wikimedia Commons. The publishers have made every effort to ensure these images are rights-free, and apologize to any creator for inadvertent unauthorized use of their image.

SLG Press
Convent of the Incarnation
Fairacres • Oxford
www.slgpress.co.uk

Printed by
Grosvenor Group Ltd, Loughton, Essex

CONTENTS

——◆——

———◦———

The author would like to thank Revd Fr James Ramsay for reading the manuscript and advising on the text. His guidance was invaluable in bringing this book to fruition.

The author and publishers acknowledge with gratitude the generous permission of the following:
Rabbi Sheila Peltz Weinberg for the reproduction of her prayer on page 43;
Revd Lionel Fanthorpe for the reproduction of his prayer-poem on pages 50–1;
The Literary Trustees of Walter de la Mare and The Society of Authors as their representative, for the reproduction of the poem by Walter de la Mare on page 77.

DOORS

Prayer is the key that opens many doors.
Faith is the hand that turns it.

INTRODUCTION

In my Father's house there are many dwelling places.

(John 14:2)

This verse is variously translated, sometimes using the word 'mansions' or 'rooms' rather than 'dwelling places', but whatever the translation there is the suggestion of many doorways or thresholds between one place and another, between one person and another, or even between different ways of existing.

Many years ago, before and after I entered community, I experienced a recurring dream: I was going up a stairway with stone steps and every few steps I came to a door which I opened, and on I continued, up the stairway. Gradually the steps got steeper and the doorways narrower, until I simply could not squeeze through them, no matter much I tried. Then of course I would wake, tired out with the struggle.

This went on at intervals; then I was professed and that night the dream came again, but the steps were regular and the doors of a uniform size until I emerged into a room full of golden light and crowds of people. I have never had that dream again.

It was from that time that I began to meditate on doors. Thinking of that quotation from the Gospel of John makes me think of many doors, and each could need a key. The key that opens these doors is prayer, and what a gift that is. This book is about using prayer to open doors within ourselves, in others and between ourselves and those around us, doors that lead us, ultimately to God.

PRAYER: THE KEY THAT OPENS MANY DOORS

Prayer is a key to heaven's storehouse, but faith unlocks the door.
A prayer without faith is like a key without a hand to turn it.

Charles Capps (1934–2014)

It is important to think about prayer as a God-given gift. Our part is to be there for God, ready and willing to give God time every day, quite specifically for prayer. Just to be still and silently waiting; as the psalmist writes:

For God alone my soul waits in silence;
from him comes my salvation.   (Ps. 62:1)

How often do we stop to think of prayer as a gift? A gift from God to His people, for all people. All people are His, believers and unbelievers alike. For some people prayer is a regular and important part of life whatever their situation, while for others it is missing. People have all sorts of reasons for not praying: don't pray, can't pray, won't pray.

Don't pray: don't know what to say; don't really have time; don't go to church.

Can't pray: I'm not really good enough; prayer is all right for experts, specialists, 'professional praying people' like priests, monks or nuns.

Won't pray: I don't believe it works; I tried once but gave up when I did not get any answers.

All this feels very true for those who have these reasons not to pray: they have virtually closed all of the doors in my metaphor. I think perhaps we have all done that at some time. But there is another way:

Not knowing when the dawn will come, I open every door.

Emily Dickinson (1830–1886)

A door usually leads us into different places and offers new opportunities and fresh encounters. Most people seek something beyond themselves, regardless of whether they acknowledge it or recognize their search. When I think of prayer as the key that opens many doors—as in the quotation right at the beginning of this book—I recognize that the object of my search is God. When we wait on God in prayer, in contemplation, we do not know what He has in store for us. We persevere in faith, giving time to God in prayer and leave the rest to Him. His is the doing; ours the being, the listening.

Doors represent margins or thresholds, and these are at the edges, not in the middle of a space. Jesus was often on the edge of society: how often He withdrew to the periphery, into the desert, away from the crowds to be alone with God. Jesus showed us His need of those times apart and, in so doing, showed us our own need for times of quiet. We need retreats: moments to stop and reflect, moments of silent adoration, if we are to be His followers today. I have written about these doors into a prayerful life in the chapters that follow.

> In the gospel we see how, when Jesus was going to pray, he would often separate from the others and take himself off to some lonely place, a mountain or a desert ... Anyone who tries to pray will often start by going off somewhere in search of a little solitude or silence. Solitude does not lie outside the world. It is a product of our world and inseparable from it.
>
> André Louf (1929–2010)

Endeavouring to live a life of prayer amid the many calls upon our time, we probably communicate more than we realize, or will ever know, of the love of God for all His people, simply by the life we lead. Doors are opened with prayer!

Ponder

Our opening and Your entering are one. You knock and wait and when we open, we find that You were there along and will not leave us. Your heart opens to us with a single undivided love.

Based on the writings of Meister Eckhart (*c.* 1260–*c.* 1328)

THE CHURCH

Let each person wreathe the door of his heart so that the Holy Spirit may delight in that door, enter in and take up residence there: then by the Spirit we will be made holy.

Ephraem the Syrian (*c*. 306–373)

From small country churches and chapels to great cathedrals, in every case one gains entrance by a door; doors as varied as the buildings. But is the door also not a kind of watershed? Especially if we remember that as we pass through a doorway we leave something behind and enter something new. Or, if you like, *take off the old and put on the new* (cf. Eph. 4:22–4). Often our attitudes, behaviour and thoughts change while passing through a doorway without our even being aware of it, whether because we are making an entrance or making an exit, but mostly because, subconsciously we encompass a change when passing through a portal between one place and another.

I was glad when they said to me, "Let us go to the house of the Lord!" (Ps. 122:1)

When we say we are glad to go into the house of the Lord, what do we mean? The answer will probably be expressed differently by every person we ask. The door of prayer and praise is not one that we pass through suddenly. We do not instantly arrive with God. Passing through the doorway from our everyday lives to communion with God is something that is ongoing when giving time specifically to Him in prayer and praise, and in listening to Him speaking to us through the Scriptures, through the words of a preacher or in hymns and music. While in a place of worship we may well spend time alone, waiting upon God in awe, wonder and adoration, and in the silence steadfastly listening to discern His will for us. We cannot leave everything behind when we pass through a door, but we can gradually become aware of, and be drawn into, a different atmosphere. How we react will depend, to a great extent, on the degree of our awareness and openness.

> People do not always walk through the church door on the tip-toe of expectation, bursting with praise and wholly open for the Spirit to pour in. Neither do they arrive feeling like a congregation, an assembly. They arrive as individuals.
>
> Bishop Michael Perham (1947–2017)

The attitude we bring to our place of worship, to the Office or the Eucharist, will naturally affect our worship and what we give to it, and whether we accept or reject what God offers to us. We may not consciously be rejecting anything, but if we are out of sorts with ourselves, others and God, then we lack the grace to receive God and His mercy. Only a conscious act of contrition and a firm resolve to begin afresh can put us back on the right path. By the grace of God this is always possible, for God is love.

Let us pray with thanksgiving for every door to worship that opens for us: for our church, chapel, abbey, cathedral; for our freedom to worship in the House of God. Let us also pray for those who are denied this freedom yet remain steadfast in the faith.

Ponder

Thanks be to thee, my Lord Jesus Christ,
for all the benefits thou hast given me,
for all the pains and insults thou hast borne for me.
O most merciful redeemer, friend and brother,
may I know thee more clearly,
love thee more dearly,
and follow thee more nearly.
Amen

St Richard of Chichester (1245–1253)

THE HOUSEHOLD OF GOD

O God, make the door of this house wide enough to receive all who need human love and fellowship, narrow enough to shut out all envy, pride and strife. Make its threshold smooth enough to be no stumbling-block to children, nor to straying feet, but rugged and strong enough to turn back the tempter's power. God make the door of this house the gateway to Thine eternal kingdom.

Prayer on the door of Saint Stephen's Church, London

For a day in your courts is better than a thousand elsewhere.
I would rather be a doorkeeper in the house of my God than
live in the tents of wickedness.   (Ps. 84:10)

We can all recall moments in our life when a door has opened and then closed behind us and a new phase in our life has begun: our first day at school, moving house, going to college, starting a new job, first steps as a committed Christian arriving at a new church or, for a few, those first steps into a consecrated life. We may remember standing at the door, about to cross the threshold and perhaps wondering whether to knock or ring the bell, or whether to turn tail and go home again. But God brought us here whether we wish it or not. Those who enter through the door come in answer to God's call. God calls us and prompts in us a hunger to know Him more fully, to increase our love for Him and all people, and to live our lives totally for Him and His Glory. We are part of the church and, as such, part of the household of God.

> Everloving Lord, source and fountain of all love, you have commanded us to love each other as you have loved us. Grant us your peace so that we may become one in heart and mind. Inspire and empower us to grow together in fullness of life within your household.
>
> Prayer for Christian Unity, 1995

Just to stand at the door of the House of God,
    steadfast in purpose,
      strong in faith,
        filled with praise,
          waiting upon God,
            listening for His voice,
              ready and eager to do His will
                with the spirit of love working through us,
                  can fill us with unspeakable joy and peace.
The door stands open, inviting us to enter and share the richness of God's goodness and grace that awaits us. Faith will let us pass through that door. If we remain steadfast in faith, and glad too, we have nothing to fear and much to gain. For God alone is our strength; He takes us as we are, with our strengths and our weaknesses, and uses us for His own good purposes.

This can be a surprise to us, or even dismay us. Only with hindsight can we say, yes, that was the right decision for that particular moment in time, and be thankful. Indeed, how thankful we need to be, always, that God in His mercy, in His love, prompts and guides and saves us from many a fall if we listen to Him and obey cheerfully. I sometimes think that many of our moments of lack of enthusiasm for life, our lethargy, our seeming lack of joy, are due to our reluctance, hesitancy, backwardness in being thankful.

It is the prayer of Fellowship which gives expression to the Common Life, ideally it binds all into oneness before God as with one heart and voice as a Community we glorify God. The tribute of the Divine Office is a tribute of many notes, but all rise in one outpouring of praises before the Throne of Glory, so we must give our best attention to the recitation and singing which represents the Eternal praise of the Eternal Word of the Father.

It is Christ's prayer, who though He was God, yet prayed as man and used the words of the psalter. Jesus is present: 'Where two or three are gathered in my name there am I in their midst.' It is the prayer of the whole church.

Fr Lucius Cary SSJE (1866–1950)

So let us give thanks for our Office, for the church, the household of God.

Lord, we beseech Thee to keep Thy household the Church in continual godliness: that through Thy protection it may be free from all adversities and devoutly given to serve Thee in all good works, to the Glory of Thy Name. Amen.

Book of Common Prayer

Ponder

Do I hesitate on the threshold, or do I walk forward into the communion of God's household?

THE WAY AND OUR RESPONSE

The Lord is my Pace-setter, I shall not rush;
He makes me stop and rest for quiet intervals.
He provides me with images of stillness,
which restore my serenity.
He leads me in ways of efficiency
through calmness of mind,
and His guidance is peace.
Even though I have a great many things
to accomplish each day, I will not fret,
for His presence is here;
His timelessness, His all-importance,
will keep me in balance.
He prepares refreshment and renewal
in the midst of my activity
by anointing my mind
with His oils of tranquillity.
My cup of joyous energy overflows.
Surely harmony and effectiveness
shall be the fruits of my hours;
for I shall walk, in the pace of my Lord
and dwell in His house forever.

Toki Miyashina

I am the door: by me if any man enter in, he shall be saved,
and shall go in and out, and find pasture.   (John 10:9 KJV)

Jesus proclaims that He is the door. He is the door that is ever
open, ever inviting us to go in and feed on the pastures of the
Word of God, upheld by the love of God the Father, in the en-
abling strength of God the Holy Spirit.

I have set before you an open door that no one is able to shut.
(Rev. 3:8)

How often we stand in the doorway longing to go through, yet not wanting to leave the known for the unknown; afraid of what that may entail and, indeed, unwilling to pay the price. Foolish mortals! Nothing is gained without giving.

> Through the unknown, remembered gate
> When the last of earth left to discover
> Is that which was the beginning;
> At the source of the longest river
> The voice of the hidden waterfall
> And the children in the apple-tree
> Not known, because not looked for
> But heard, half-heard, in the stillness
> Between two waves of the sea.
> Quick now, here, now, always—
> A condition of complete simplicity
> (Costing not less than everything)
> And all shall be well and
> All manner of thing shall be well.
>
> T. S. Eliot (1888–1965)

Only that which costs *not less than everything* is worth having; that which demands the total commitment of our whole selves — body, mind and spirit — given in love to love, receiving love, and all to the glory of the God of Love who gives unlimited love to those who, in obedience, enter by the door.

> One of the images that ... speaks volumes to me is the one of Christ the door, the keeper of the gate. Very often when I pray or meditate, gazing at the large icon of the Lord in our chapel, I get a clear and distinct understanding that Christ is truly the door through which we must all pass to come to the Father. As I focus on that precise icon day after day, I see an open door through which I must go to enter deeply into God.
>
> Brother Victor-Antoine d'Avila-Latourrette OSB

Let us pray with thanksgiving for the knowledge that Jesus is the Door, the Way, the Truth and the Life; for God's love for us, and for the gift of the Holy Spirit.

Ponder

Pray for all who are seeking to know God;
For those who feel lost and bewildered;
For all who seek to help others along the Way.

THE DOOR OF ACCEPTANCE

> Listen! I am standing at the door, knocking; if you hear my
> voice and open the door, I will come in to you and eat with
> you, and you with me. (Rev. 3:20)

The sound of knocking, someone calling … Would we at once
recognize the Lord? We might well be like Samuel and go once
or twice to see who was calling, before we could decide, 'Yes, it
is the Lord, and then with Samuel we can say to the Lord:
"Speak, for your servant is listening" (1 Sam. 3:10). This is only
the beginning. There is more to come in the waiting, the listening
and the obeying:

> For God alone my soul waits in silence,
> for my hope is from him.
> He alone is my rock and my salvation,
> my fortress; I shall not be shaken.
> On God rests my deliverance and my honour;
> my mighty rock, my refuge is in God.
> Trust in him at all times, O people;
> pour out your heart before him; God is a refuge for us.
> (Ps. 62:5–8)

It may be that the Lord is showing us how to cope with some problem or difficulty that has been causing us anxiety and soul-searching; we would be so thankful to know the way forward and probably eager to get started. On the other hand, perhaps the Lord is showing us some particular failure in poverty, humility, charity or lack of love and understanding. Yes, we ought to be glad to be made aware of this; but our more likely action, because of our human frailty, may be to close the door of our hearts in rejection or anger. We do not like to be told the truth about ourselves at the moment of its telling. Given time for reflection, though, we come to appreciate the value of this insight, accept it, and firmly resolve to make amends. That is not easy, but God in His great mercy makes it possible.

How often we need to pray: *God, make me willing to be willing to do your will*, again and again and again. In our hearts we do want to welcome Jesus: to love, to serve, to come and worship, and adore in songs of everlasting praise.

> The Father and I will come and make our home with him. Let your door be open to Him when He comes, open your soul, throw open your inmost mind, so that it may see the riches of simplicity, the treasures of peace, the sweetness of grace. Open your heart, melt the sun of eternal light that enlightens every man. The true light indeed shines on all, but if everyone has closed his windows, he will rob himself of eternal light. Christ, too, is shut out if you close the door of your mind. Although He is able to enter, He does not wish to rush in uninvited. He does not wish to force the entry. Blessed is the man at whose door Christ knocks. Our door is faith, which if it is strong fortifies the whole house. It is through this door that Christ comes in.
>
> St Ambrose (*c.*339–*c.*397)

We are often reluctant to open the door of our inner selves; that which is more difficult to share:

> Lord we thank you for continuing to knock at our door. Help us to open at your call. Help us to listen to the words you now wish

to speak in our hearts. We have been restless, trying to accomplish our self-imposed tasks, setting aside your word, and going our own way. Lord, give us the courage to act. But let all that we do derive from your living Word. Amen.

Prayer for Christian Unity, 1996

God knocks, He nudges. We feel that inner nudge: God saying, "Come on, I want you to do this or that for me." Yes, we are aware, but our response may be slow.

Sometimes we shut God out, perhaps because it is too difficult to let Him in, or perhaps we have given up or we feel shame for something we have done. But we can remember that if Jesus wants to be with us, even closing the door is not a barrier to Him.

A week later his disciples were again in the house, and Thomas was with them. Although the doors were shut, Jesus came and stood among them and said, "Peace be with you."
(John 20:26)

When we do make a positive response, let us do it with joy and thanksgiving for the glory of God. Let us give thanks that the Lord does knock; that He speaks, if we will listen and obey.

The door of my heart is closed,
The barriers are put right across,
Nothing, no one shall enter,
Nothing disturbs my oasis.
Yet still You visit and implore
Until all barriers come down
And Yes – I can say welcome!
There is room in my heart for Thee.

Anon.

Ponder

God often visits us, but most of the time we are not at home.

Joseph Roux (1834–1905)

THE DOOR OF HOPE

From there I will give her her vineyards, and make the Valley
of Achor a door of hope.   (Hos. 2:15)

A door of hope. A welcome in the desert. An encouragement
along the way; an affirmation that something is right for a given
moment in time, or equally is ill-advised for that moment. All
these give us hope and point us to the next step.

Hope is something we all need, though it is not always ob-
vious, and sometimes feels like a mystery. No words can really
describe what hope is, yet our experience tells us what is hopeful, and our inmost being—that spirit within us—responds with

hope in so many ways. Perhaps hope is best described in prayer as that deep fellowship with Christ from which springs the hope of eternal life; that eager looking forward in gladness so indescribable because it is to God, the hope of all the world.

> Look well to this day for it is life,
> The very life of life!
> …
> For yesterday is but a dream and tomorrow is only a vision.
> For today well-lived makes every yesterday a dream of happiness,
> And every tomorrow a vision of hope.
> Look well therefore to this day.
>
> Kalidasa (4th–6th century AD)

How important each day is, and how important it is to live each day for God.

> Blessed be the God and Father of our Lord Jesus Christ! By his great mercy he has given us a new birth into a living hope through the resurrection of Jesus Christ from the dead.
>
> (1 Pet. 1:3)

St Peter puts it in a nutshell: our hope is in the resurrection, the promise of eternal life for all who follow God and give their lives to Him. After the Resurrection all the disciples were filled with hope, and this colours everything that come after. St Paul wrote this to the Ephesians:

> There is one body and one Spirit, just as you were called to the one hope of your calling.
>
> (Eph. 4:4)

The hope of salvation was something that Paul wrote of many times in his letters sent to support the faith of the isolated new Christian communities. He reassured them and encouraged them to look forward in gladness, beyond their present difficulties and the persecution that they suffered.

> Therefore, since we are justified by faith, we have peace with God through our Lord Jesus Christ, through whom we have obtained access to this grace in which we stand; and we boast

in our hope of sharing the glory of God. And not only that, but we also boast in our sufferings, knowing that suffering produces endurance, and endurance produces character, and character produces hope, and hope does not disappoint us, because God's love has been poured into our hearts through the Holy Spirit that has been given to us.   (Rom. 5:1–5)

There is always hope in whatever situation we find ourselves, if we keep our minds looking towards God. We need to be hopeful, expectant people.

We hear so much about those who are without hope, who despair of things ever being hopeful; but we can hope for life eternal in the fullness of time, and pray for those who have lost hope, and have compassion for them.

Fr Gilbert Shaw writes that hope and prayer should be a steady knocking, rather than an insistent barrage:

> there should not be a 'banging on the door', for this is both self-expressive and a disturbance to recollection. We must learn to wait in the simple confidence of faith.
>
> Fr Gilbert Shaw (1886–1967)

If we are hopeful, expectant, joyful, then surely others will see that in us, for we witness to our faith. Let us give thanks for God's gift of hope to us, and pray for those who have lost hope.

Ponder

All my hope on God is founded;
He doth still my trust renew.
Me through change and chance He guideth,
Only good and only true.
God unknown,
He alone
calls my heart to be His own.

Joachim Neander (1650–1680),
trans. Robert Bridges (1844–1930)

THE DOOR OF SIN

If you do well, will you not be accepted? And if you do not do
well, sin is lurking at the door; its desire is for you, but you
must master it.   (Gen. 4:7)

That is rather a blunt statement, but we often need to be told
things simply and bluntly to make us sit up and take notice.

Chapter 7 of Genesis tells the story of Cain and Abel, of
Cain's jealousy of his brother being more in favour with the
Lord than himself, as he saw it. Such was his jealousy that it led
him to kill his brother—a sad and drastic end to the sin of jealousy. Drastic and unlovely. But what about all the little unlovely
things we do in the course of a day? The angry word, the ugly
look, the 'forgotten' task, the error ignored; works that lack kindness, moments of selfishness, uncharitable or judgmental
thoughts. All of these show a lack of love.

Little things, yes, but little things grow to big things if we do
not acknowledge and deal with them while they are still small,
so that they cannot grow and become something worse, to our
sorrow and shame. There is a very apt saying of one of the
Desert Fathers that sums up temptation to sin in thought, word
and deed:

If you had a door and shut it, and did not let the evil thoughts
come through it, then you would see them standing outside
warring against you.

From the *Apophthegmata Patrum* (*c.* 5th century)

Today, so much sadness, unrest and war seems to be all
about the struggle for power, possessions and money, at the
expense of other people's lives. Keeping the door to sin closed
can be difficult, and more difficult the more we have come to
love our possessions and our status. But we know that God

loves us just as we are, in all our frailty and, by the grace of God, we can be helped to keep the door of sin closed. We pray to God for the strength to protect us and keep us from sin, to deliver us from evil.

Ponder

Does my door stand open to sin?

THE DOOR OF HUMILITY, PENITENCE
& FORGIVENESS

Gracious Lord,
you have given us the privilege of an open door to
    your presence.
When life is shining and full, inhabit our joy.
When life is grinding slowly on, touch us with your life.
When we long for clearer vision of you, open our
    gauze-covered eyes.
When we studiously avoid your gaze, tempt us with
    your forgiving smile.
Lead us inexorably to the fulfilment of our lives in the
    service of your Son,
so that, dipped in God and cherished by your Spirit,
we may come to you, three times blessed,
Father, Son and Holy Spirit.
Amen.

Bishop John Pritchard

As a door turns on its hinges, so does a lazy person in bed.
(Prov. 26:14)

What a fascinating image, and how true. Do we not sometimes turn to and fro as a door swings on its hinges, just as uselessly as a swinging door? Lacking in purpose and stability—simply putting off the moment of doing. Is that how we hover on the doorstep of the door that is Christ? We hover, wanting to enter, yet somewhere within us is an unwillingness to take that step of love. Self is all too important and earthly things loom large until we can truly pray: *Lord, take me, break me, make me Thine*; and so let go and let God in.

God, in His infinite love, never asks anything of us that is beyond us if we trust Him for help and guidance and do all to

His praise and glory. We know that if we come to Him in penitence, He will forgive us and help us to begin again.

> A sinner who begins to show concern over his soul and who becomes penitent is like a kitchen utensil which is full of filth and blackened, yet once washed and scrubbed it glistens. Again he resembles a piece of charcoal that was dark coloured and cold, but when it is put on the fire it becomes hot and glows. Have a love for penitence then, put your neck under its yoke. Give pleasure to your Lord by changing from bad actions to good. Be reconciled readily, while there is still time, while you have authority over your soul.
>
> Evagrius Ponticus (*c.* 346–399)

How ready and willing are we to put our necks under the yoke of penitence? There are constant calls to repentance in the New Testament, but often it is easier to travel along in the comfortable rut we know than to make an effort to change. Nonetheless we may well come to a pothole on the way that will give us a much-needed jolt. However unpleasant the jolt, the outcome is likely to be good and stimulating in its long-term effect. A means of going deeper into some aspect of our lives, learning more about ourselves, and giving us an uncomfortable time.

We may become more aware of the tremendous amount of suffering in the world today and our part in it, and try to admit this more fully as we bring it to Christ in penitence, remembering the agony in Gethsemane and His suffering on the Cross for our redemption. But God forgives us, and bids us forgive others in our turn.

> Forgiveness is the key that unlocks the door of resentment and the handcuffs of hate. It is a power that breaks the chains of bitterness and the shackles of selfishness. He who cannot forgive others, breaks the bridge over which he himself must pass.
>
> Corrie ten Boom (1892–1983)

We could replace the word 'Forgiveness' in this quotation with 'Prayer', and as we pray we examine all that we have done and the effect of those actions on others.

> When evening comes, collect your thoughts and ponder over the entire course of the day: observe God's providential care for you; consider the grace he has wrought in you throughout the whole span of the day; ... When you have pondered on all this, wonder of God's love towards you will well up within you, and gratitude for his acts of grace will bubble up inside you.
>
> Take thought too, in case you have done something that is contrary to these acts of grace: say to yourself 'Have I done anything to anger God today? Have I said or thought anything that does not befit that will which created me?' And if you become aware that you have done something to displease him, stand up for a short while in prayer and give thanks for the graces you have received throughout the entire day's ministry, and make supplication for what you have done wrong. In this way you will sleep peacefully and without sin.
>
> ...
>
> Such then should be your daily aim throughout life, each morning you should look back on your service during the night and each evening look back on your service during the day. Complete your ways thus in purity in accordance with the will of God.
>
> John 'the Solitary' of Apamea (*fl.* early 5th century)

Swinging to and fro like the door, we look back and forth, not idly like the door in Proverbs, but to some purpose. We examine our past and look to the future and resolve to serve the Lord more nearly with our whole selves: body, mind and spirit. In the seventh century one of the Desert Fathers, Isaac of Nineveh, wrote a number of 'discourses' to explain the evolving ideas of a life given wholly to God for those who were interested in leading a life of asceticism and penitence.

The sum of the entire ascetic course consists in these three things: repentance, purity, and perfection. What is repentance? Desisting from former sins, and feeling pain at them. What is purity, in a nutshell? a heart which has compassion on every natural thing in creation. What is perfection? Profound humility.

…

Another time the same Father was asked: What is repentance? He answered: A broken heart.

Isaac of Nineveh (c. 613–c. 700)

Repentance is—or should be—a matter of sorrow coupled with a resolve to do better. What about the Sacrament of Penance today?

What seems to be undeniable is that contemporary Christians focus much more upon the God of forgiveness and Love who is revealed in Jesus Christ, rather than on the God of vengeance and judgement, who is no less to be found in the pages of Scripture. I for one, believe that our contemporary concentration upon forgiveness does greater justice to the teaching of Jesus.

Bishop George Carey

We each have to do what is right for us at any given time; it will not always be the same pattern, and certainly will be different for different people. What matters is that we have some definite pattern or Rule and adhere to it for as long as it serves, then be ready to make adjustments as necessary.

The door swings to and fro, so while we may be pointed to repentance, we may also be shown some new thing. A new dimension in prayer, a new field of study, some new ideas to think about. These growth points, like new buds on a twig, need nurturing, so that they may grow and flower. They need to be nurtured with love, our love and encouragement for each other and God's everlasting love for us all.

O Christ, the ocean of our forgiveness, allow me to wash off in you the dirt that I am clothed in, that I may become resplendent in the raiment of your Holy Light.

John of Dalyatha (c. 690–c. 780)

Banished from the joys of paradise,
Adam sat outside and wept
and beating his hand upon his face, he said,
"I am fallen, in your compassion, have mercy on me."

When Adam saw the angel drive him out
and shut the door of the divine garden,
he groaned aloud and said:
"I am fallen, in your compassion, have mercy on me."

From the Hymn for the Sunday of Forgiveness

The Sunday of Forgiveness is the last Sunday before the commencement of Great Lent in the Orthodox Church. On this day the focus is on the exile of Adam and Eve from the Garden of Eden, an event that shows us how far we have fallen in sin and separated ourselves from God. As the great period of Lenten fasting begins, this Sunday reminds us of our need for God's forgiveness. It helps to focus the heart, mind, and spiritual efforts on returning to Him in repentance.

Ponder

Look well, O soul, upon thyself
lest spiritual ambition
should mislead and blind thee
to thy essential task —
to wait in quietness:
to knock and persevere in humble faith.
Knock thou in love, nor fail to keep thy place before the door
that when Christ wills — and not before — he shall open unto
thee the treasures of his love.

Grant me humility of soul
that I may grow in penitence
dependent on the Holy Spirit's light.

Fr Gilbert Shaw (1886–1967)

THE DOOR OF COMPASSION

Oh Lord, make me an instrument of Thy Peace!
Where there is hatred, let me sow love.
Where there is injury, pardon.
Where there is discord, harmony.
Where there is despair, hope.
Where there is darkness, light.
Where there is sorrow, joy.
Oh Master, grant that I may not
so much seek to be consoled as to console;
to be understood as to understand;
to be loved as to love;
for it is in giving that we receive;
it is in pardoning that we are pardoned;
and it is in dying that we are born to Eternal Life.

St Francis of Assisi (*c.*1181–1226)

The stranger has not lodged in the street; I have opened my
doors to the traveller.   (Job 31:32)

We know what this means in practical terms, and we have mixed
feelings about what it is right to do when someone comes to the
door wanting money, tea and sandwiches, a blanket, or even
hoping for somewhere quiet to sleep. One is reminded of

Matthew 25:37–40: when did we see you, hungry or thirsty, naked or sick, or a homeless person on the pavement? Sadly in our world today we know that for every genuine case there are several that are not, and it is not always easy to discern those whose need is genuine. People expect a sympathetic hearing from the church—priests, monks, nuns, the Salvation Army—plus some practical help. The regular 'Gentlemen of the Road'—and they do seem to be mostly men—seldom ask for more than a cup of tea. How much are we serving God in what we do for these people? Do we have compassion for them and hold them up to God for His love and mercy? In his first Hymn on the Nativity St Ephraem tells us that because the gates of heaven have been opened to us, we should also open our doors to those who ask for forgiveness.

> This is the day that opened for us a gate on high to our prayers.
> Let us open also gates to supplicants that have transgressed, and
> of us have asked [forgiveness].
>
> Ephraem the Syrian (*c.* 306–373)

Compassion seems to be singularly lacking in those people who are the perpetrators of so much violence and suffering in the world. Against that, one can set those many people who work so hard for the suffering and deprived peoples of the world, often in a voluntary capacity. Through their work they are reaching out with compassion for those whom they seek to help.

> Compassion is the gate by which the saints enter into the knowl-
> edge of God. You should realise brother, that whenever
> movements of compassion are stirred in you, they are insights
> into the spiritual understanding of judgment and knowledge.
>
> From the *Apophthegmata Patrum* (*c.* 5th century)

We cannot all travel to the regions of the world where urgent help is necessary, nor even house our own deprived, and home-less, but we can show our compassion for all those in need throughout the world by our prayers, by trying to see Christ in them and continually holding them up to God.

But to share with Christ Jesus his Passion, his Crucifixion, his death means to accept unreservedly all these events in the same spirit as he did, that is, to accept them in an act of free will, to suffer together with the man of sorrows, to be there in silence, the silence of real communion; not just the silence of pity, but of compassion which allows us to grow into complete oneness with the other so that there is no longer one and the other, but only one life and one death.

Metropolitan Anthony Bloom (1914–2003)

Is that not how we need to enter into human suffering too? By accepting and acknowledging that we are part of it and offering it, and ourselves, to God. Entering into the compassion of Christ and being taken into Him.

Soul of Christ sanctify me,
Body of Christ save me,
Blood of Christ inebriate me,
Water from the side of Christ wash me,
Passion of Christ strengthen me.
O good Jesu hear me,
Within Thy wounds hide me,
Suffer me not to be separated from Thee,
From the malicious enemy defend me,
In the hour of my death call me,
And bid me come to Thee.
That with thy saints I may praise Thee,
For ever and ever. Amen.

Ponder

And the king will answer them, "Truly I tell you, just as you did it to one of the least of these who are members of my family, you did it to me." (Matt. 25:40)

THE DOOR OF STUDY

Wisdom is radiant and unfading,
and she is easily discerned by those who love her,
and is found by those who seek her.
She hastens to make herself known to those who desire her.
One who rises early to seek her will have no difficulty,
for she will be found sitting at the gate.
To fix one's thought on her is perfect understanding,
and one who is vigilant on her account will soon be free from care,
because she goes about seeking those worthy of her,
and she graciously appears to them in their paths,
and meets them in every thought. (Wis. 6:12–16)

Study is the door into wisdom. We study to gain knowledge, to widen our outlook on life, to increase our understanding of Scripture, to help us come nearer to comprehending something of the mystery of God. Maybe also for simple enjoyment, for pleasure. For some it may be to enable them to preach, to teach, to write with more authority—with confidence and trust in the Lord and what they say about Him.

Study may well help us to a more intelligent reading and understanding about faith and mission. We may also use study to keep our minds alert, but study is also a means of following the Way, the example set by earlier Christians.

What do we study? The Bible, the Lives of the Saints, religious traditions, biographies, religious and spiritual writers and biblical commentators throughout the ages, from the Desert Fathers and Mothers to contemporary spiritual leaders—to suggest but a few.

How shall we begin? With prayer, always dedicating the time to God. Ask advice and suggestions for reading from a spiritual director, priest, friend, monastic, and act on it: and then get down to work!

We need to be disciplined in giving time regularly for concentrated periods of study, or we can become dispirited at our lack of progress, and perhaps give up. On the other hand we can become so engrossed in study that it becomes our top priority, putting other aspects of life in the shade—that is a real danger.

Those who have a gift for writing should use it. We should also encourage anyone we know with such a gift to write for others, seeking always the wisdom of God and doing all to His glory.

Ponder

My child, if you accept my words
and treasure up my commandments within you,
making your ear attentive to wisdom
and inclining your heart to understanding;
if you indeed cry out for insight,
and raise your voice for understanding;
if you seek it like silver,
and search for it as for hidden treasures—
then you will understand the fear of the Lord
and find the knowledge of God.
For the Lord gives wisdom;
from his mouth come knowledge and understanding;
he stores up sound wisdom for the upright;
he is a shield to those who walk blamelessly,
guarding the paths of justice
and preserving the way of his faithful ones.
Then you will understand righteousness and justice
and equity, every good path;
for wisdom will come into your heart,
and knowledge will be pleasant to your soul;
prudence will watch over you;
and understanding will guard you.   (Prov. 2:1–11)

THE DOOR OF WORK

> For the entrance to the inner sanctuary he made doors of olivewood; the lintel and the doorposts were five-sided. He covered the two doors of olivewood with carvings of cherubim, palm trees, and open flowers; he overlaid them with gold, and spread gold on the cherubim and on the palm trees. So also he made for the entrance to the nave doorposts of olivewood, four-sided each, and two doors of cypress wood; the two leaves of the one door were folding, and the two leaves of the other door were folding. He carved cherubim, palm trees, and open flowers, overlaying them with gold evenly applied upon the carved work. (1 Kings 6:31–4)

This passage from the first Book of Kings about making the doors for the Temple is striking for the level of detail recorded. The story of Solomon's building of the Temple is rich in such specifics. When we meditate on this, we recall how everything had to be done manually; with just a few simple, hand-made tools. How hard all those hundreds of people must have worked to obtain the necessary wood and stone, and the builders themselves using all their energy and strength, day after day, to make a solid and enduring structure for the Temple, all the while knowing that they might not live long enough to see the completed building.

All of these different craftsmen and labourers were working to build as a team, each depending on the other. Is that not like a true Church community? Each with responsibility to do well whatever their vocation may entail; with care, joy and love.

> Teach me, my God and King,
> In all things Thee to see,
> And what I do in anything,
> To do it as for Thee.
>
> George Herbert (1593–1633)

That is not so difficult when we are doing work which we enjoy, but it is sometimes another story when we have a task that we do not enjoy, and struggle to complete; then it is harder to do it all for God cheerfully.

Why should this be so? Is it perhaps the desire to do only those things that we know we can succeed in, our pride wanting always to be successful? This holds us back, and it is why we avoid the difficult things, thus letting the devil have his way, and so we fail.

> Strive to enter through the narrow door; for many, I tell you,
> will try to enter and will not be able. (Luke 13:24)

We need not despair, for by the grace of God we can acknowledge our failures, our lack of trust, our selfishness, our pride, or whatever is our particular stumbling block, and we can begin again and make a new start.

We need the exercise that manual work provides if we are to keep healthy in body, mind and spirit, for each of these parts interacts with the others, so all parts need to be well if the whole person is to be well. Interleaved like the parts of the Temple doors.

We can enjoy our work and get into our own rhythm, and contemplate while working if we give ourselves wholly to the task in hand without worrying about the next thing, or whether we shall have time for whatever other things are in our lives or thoughts; that uses up such a lot of energy to no purpose. So let us work steadily, prayerfully and cheerfully, and to the glory of God.

Ponder

Turn your eyes upon Jesus,
Look full in His wonderful face,
And the things of earth will grow strangely dim,
In the light of His glory and grace.

Helen Howarth Lemmel (1863–1961)

THE DOOR OF RECREATION

> David and all the house of Israel were dancing before the Lord
> with all their might, with songs and lyres and harps and
> tambourines and castanets and cymbals.   (2 Sam. 6:5)

This verse, although not about recreation, is about celebration
following a time of war and uncertainty. It communicates a
sense of freedom and joy that are surely the keynote of recreation. The ability to celebrate and relax is one that we should not
neglect. Recreation should be time spent doing something that
is at least creative, relaxing or stimulating—and which gives us
a sense of wellbeing and joy. We all need some recreation time,
however we spend it. The Bible is filled with descriptions of
people resting, acknowledging that rest is necessary and important. It is perhaps more important than ever these days, that we
allow ourselves to take a break from our work and our lives,

when life is lived at such a pace and is filled with so many 'things' that require our attention.

> He said to them, "Come away to a deserted place all by yourselves and rest a while." For many were coming and going, and they had no leisure even to eat.　　(Mark 6:31)

It is up to us to give ourselves time for something we find recreational. Even a short time—as little as a quarter of an hour doing something recreational, or creative—can be rejuvenating and relaxing. We need to reserve time for this each day and, equally, to make sure it is not swallowed up by something else. So make space and *enjoy* it. The Lord did not wish us to live lives of pure work and austerity: Scripture recognizes that we cannot do our best work—and this means that we cannot make our best offering to God with our lives and our prayer—if we are too tired or distracted to give of our best.

> A hunter in the desert saw abba Antony enjoying himself with the brothers, and he was shocked. Wanting to show him that it was necessary sometimes to meet the needs of the brothers, the old man said to him, "Put an arrow in your bow and shoot it." So he did. And the old man said, "Shoot another," and he did so. Then the old man said, "Shoot yet again," and the hunter replied, "If I bend my bow so much, I will break it." Then the old man said to him, "It is the same with the work of God. If we stretch the brothers beyond measure, they will soon break. Sometimes it is necessary to come down to meet their needs."
>
> A story of Abba Antony (*d.* 356)

Ponder

A cheerful heart is a good medicine, but a downcast spirit dries up the bones.　　(Prov. 17:22)

Lift up your heads, O gates! and be lifted up, O ancient doors! that the King of glory may come in.　　(Ps. 24:7)

THE DOOR OF FASTING

Is this picture of fasting what fasting is all about? To deny ourselves food such that we come close to death's door? Are we likely to become more useful people if we do that? I think not.

Why fast at all? There are many reasons people fast, though we don't always use that word: many people fast to lose weight; some use fasting to enable them to think more clearly. As Christians we fast because it is our duty in Lent or on fasting days, and this is often accompanied by giving the money saved to charity, particularly one dedicated to alleviating hunger. Sometimes we fast to remind ourselves not to let the demands of our bodies govern us, and sometimes because we wish to give something up for God.

In the Old Testament and the early Christian church, fasting was most often associated with penitence. But in the New Testament, fasting is often presented as a way of strengthening prayer. When Paul and Barnabas are appointing elders for the chruch in Iconium and Antioch, Acts 4:3 says that they are entrusting them to the Lord with prayer and fasting.

St Augustine believed, and preached, that fasting without almsgiving is pointless, and the tradition of fasting in order to give to others is one that has been deeply embedded in the Christian tradition for centuries.

This is what human righteousness consists of in this life: fasting, almsgiving and prayer. Do you want your prayer to fly to God? Then make two wings for it, fasting and almsdeeds.

St Augustine (354–430)

Why do Christians fast? There are several reasons:
 –To bring ourselves nearer to the sufferings of Christ;
 –To increase our compassion for others and be concerned for their needs;
 –To bring us into a deeper relationship with God;
 –To help our growth in prayer;
 –To help us in Lent to prepare to enter into the Passion of Christ and the events of Holy Week, that we may be better prepared to rejoice with Alleluias on Easter Day.

In the Gospels we read of Jesus spending forty days in the wilderness as a preparation for His ministry here on earth, a fast that we recall during the forty days of Lent. It is a period to aid our preparation for Holy Week and Easter, a time to give ourselves to prayer and fasting, to deny ourselves some foods, to restrict our appetites, to exercise self-discipline. But this is only one kind of fasting.

We might look at some of our bad habits and endeavour to give them up entirely, not just for Lent: self-pleasing things that get in the way of growth in prayer and our church commitments and conduct at work. Isaiah chapter 58 gives us a good guide for fasting and what pleases the Lord and, although it is a long passage, I offer it in full here. When we hold fasting in all its facets in the right perspective, then the Lord, in His great compassion, will be our guide and friend.

Is not this the fast that I choose: to loose the bonds of injustice, to undo the thongs of the yoke, to let the oppressed go free, and to break every yoke? Is it not to share your bread with the hungry, and bring the homeless poor into your house; when you see the naked, to cover them, and not to hide yourself from your own kin? Then your light shall break forth like the dawn, and your healing shall spring up quickly; your vindicator shall go before you, the glory of the Lord shall be your rear guard. Then you shall call, and the Lord will answer; you shall cry for help, and he will say, Here I am. If you remove the yoke from among you, the pointing of the finger, the speaking of evil, if you offer your food to the hungry and satisfy the needs of the afflicted, then your light shall rise in the darkness and your gloom be like the noonday. The Lord will guide you continually, and satisfy your needs in parched places, and make your bones strong; and you shall be like a watered garden, like a spring of water, whose waters never fail. Your ancient ruins shall be rebuilt; you shall raise up the foundations of many generations; you shall be called the repairer of the breach, the restorer of streets to live in.   (Is. 58:6–12)

Ponder

When I fast, do I genuinely deny myself things that I want, or only things that I feel I can do without?

THE DOOR OF THE HEART

O Lord, the door of my soul is narrow; enlarge it, that you may enter in.

St Augustine (354–430)

A certain woman named Lydia, a worshiper of God, was listening to us; she was from the city of Thyatira and a dealer in purple cloth. The Lord opened her heart to listen eagerly to what was said by Paul. (Acts 16:14)

It is a great and solemn moment when someone comes to make a deep commitment—a moment they have been preparing for, perhaps through a long process, with all of its ups and downs. There are always times of joy when all seems positive and set fair, but there are also times of doubt and questioning. Am I doing the right thing? Is this where God wants me to be?

Just as the Lord opened the door of Lydia's heart as she listened to St Paul's teaching, that she might hear and understand, so God calls us and opens the door of our hearts to His love and mercy, and we respond in faith, hope and love, with joy and thanksgiving.

> Christ leads me through no darker rooms
> Than he went through before;
> And he that in God's kingdom comes,
> Must enter by this door.

Richard Baxter (1615–1691)

So, as God brings us through the door of commitment, He will walk with us as we go forward, little knowing what the future holds for us, but confident in faith; firm in hope, and full of love for God and our sisters and brothers in Christ, upholding each other with our love and prayers. A source of strength and joy to one another.

When you discover the door of your heart you discover the gate of heaven.

St John Chrysostom (347–407)

Dear God,
open the blocked passageways to you,
the congealed places.

Roll away the heavy stone from the well
as your servant Jacob did
when he beheld his beloved Rachel.

Help us open the doors of trust
that have been jammed
with hurt and rejection.

As you open the blossoms in spring,
even
as you open the heavens in storm,

Open us –

to feel your great,
awesome,
wonderful presence

Rabbi Sheila Peltz Weinberg

Ponder

Let your door stand open to receive Christ, unlock your soul to him, offer him a welcome in your mind, and then you will see the riches of simplicity, the treasures of peace and the joy of grace. Throw wide the gate of your heart, stand before the sun of everlasting light that that shines on every one. This true light shines on all.

St Ambrose (c. 339–c. 397)

THE DOOR OF SERVICE

Lord Jesus Christ to this end, I pray: By your mercy help me to be worthy of my calling; by your power help me to fulfil my good resolves; by your grace help me to accomplish works of faith, so that your name may be glorified. Amen.

Sr Raphael

Jesus calls us and says: 'I am the Door' and 'I am the Way'. We just need to knock and enter. We each have some ministry, a gift from God, and how it is worked out will vary from person to person, from place to place, in many different situations.

The various ministries to which God sends married, celibate and single persons are also effective instruments for their personal divinization. Vocational lifestyles and ministerial pursuits interrelate to form a multifaceted but integrated vocation.

From Called by God (2001)

There it is in a nutshell, but we need to spend some time teasing it out in order to discover our own particular service or ministry, which may well change from time to time. Any service or ministry will have a common basis in prayer and the living out of the two great commandments of love for God, and love for our neighbour, as well as learning to love ourselves just as we are, with all our shortcomings.

When did we feed the hungry, welcome the stranger, visit the sick or the prisoner? We can all ask that question, for it is often the unseen, the unorganized, the unprepared moments of service to others that give glory to God. There will also be times when we can hang our heads in shame at the missed opportunities, or neglected acts of service.

We seek to listen, to pray and to obey. We all have talents, let us use them to the glory of God.

And say to Archippus, 'See that you complete the task that you
have received in the Lord.' (Col. 4:17)

The first aspect of service or ministry that I want to consider
is what I have called armchair ministry. Prayer for the world and
its many needs; offering ourselves daily to God in this service
for His glory. This is such an important service and a gift from
God to those who might otherwise feel useless. This is a ministry
which can be ongoing until the end of our days.

The other part of our ministry at home is actually about
reaching out, whether it is responding to requests for prayers,
by phone, letters, e-mail or by receiving visitors. It is part of everyone's ministry, little or much; but perhaps this home ministry
features more as we get older or less active, at a time when we
can take things into the silence of contemplation, into the silence
of God.

I am sure we all minister by reaching out to others, often
without knowing what a call has meant to someone. We keep in
touch with one another in so many ways now, and all of these
ways are part of our ministry. In the same way, being available
for people to visit and talk things over with a cup of tea or coffee,
just being a friend, can be a lifeline to someone, even if we do
not know it.

However, being available can be one of the most difficult
things, because often we do not choose the time or place, so we
have to be able to stop and turn to another person in acceptance
and readiness whenever they need us, even if it is not convenient
for us. This willingness to be available can be one of the greatest
gifts we can offer.

This you learned from Epaphras, our beloved fellow-servant.
He is a faithful minister of Christ on your behalf, and he has
made known to us your love in the Spirit. For this reason, since
the day we heard it, we have not ceased praying for you and
asking that you may be filled with the knowledge of God's
will in all spiritual wisdom and understanding, so that you

may lead lives worthy of the Lord, fully pleasing to him, as you bear fruit in every good work and as you grow in the knowledge of God. May you be made strong with all the strength that comes from his glorious power, and may you be prepared to endure everything with patience, while joyfully giving thanks to the Father, who has enabled you to share in the inheritance of the saints in the light.   (Col. 1:7–12)

The second type of service is more obviously active and visible; there are many ways in which we can offer active service to the church. We take on parish duties and activities faithfully in the service of God and to His glory, but we also need to know when to say 'No' if something is outside our abilities or if we are taking on too much. Active ministries may include things that are not specifically linked to the church, such as visiting hospitals or prisons. We must not forget the families of those in hospital or prison, who need our listening and comfort too. From our witness to God in these good works we spread His love by our example. In our prayer we say: *by your grace help me to accomplish works of faith.*

I am grateful to Christ Jesus our Lord, who has strengthened me, because he judged me faithful and appointed me to his service.
(1 Tim. 1:12)

We may never know what effect our words or actions have on others but that does not matter. Many types of service outside the church are hidden, and that is good, for Jesus told us:

Beware of practicing your piety before others in order to be seen by them; for then you have no reward from your Father in heaven. So whenever you give alms, do not sound a trumpet before you, as the hypocrites do in the synagogues and in the streets, so that they may be praised by others. Truly I tell you, they have received their reward. But when you give alms, do not let your left hand know what your right hand is doing, so that your alms may be done in secret; and your Father who sees in secret will reward you.   (Matt. 6:1–4)

But Jesus also asked us to bear witness to Him and to our faith through our good works and service:

> … let your light shine before others, so that they may see your good works and give glory to your Father in heaven.
>
> (Matt. 5:16)

Working out how to tread the path between these two extremes can be difficult, but prayer and humility can guide us.

There are so many aspects of life that we probably do not consider ministry or service, but they are. Family time is so important: families need each other and this relationship is one that admits a different type of love and listening from relationships outside family. We might feel that the demands of the family are taking us away from prayer or time with God, but we can remember that we are still serving God in our service to others. Ministry in the workplace also concerns us. Again, this is often hidden; the kind word, the friendly smile, simply being you, someone willing to listen, to be a friend.

None of these ministries could happen without prayer. The doing comes out of the prayer. This unites the Martha and Mary in us. Where would the doing be without the being?

> Christians' work, primarily through being, lies not so much in what they do or in what they allow to be done; God acting in and through them in both their effort and their prayers.
>
> From *The Spirit of Solesmes* (1997)

Ponder

> And whatever you do, in word or deed, do everything in the name of the Lord Jesus, giving thanks to God the Father through him.
>
> (Col. 3:17)

THE DOOR OF SILENCE & STILLNESS

We all have within us a centre of stillness surrounded by silence. This house, dedicated to work and debate in the service of peace, should have one room dedicated to silence in the outward sense and stillness in the inner sense. It has been the aim to create in this small room a place where the doors may be open to the infinite lands of thought and prayer.

Dag Hammarskjöld (1905–1961)

This text was written for the opening of the Meditation Room at the headquarters of the United Nations Building in New York in 1957. It was printed on a leaflet given to visitors to the Room. This quotation may remind us of a passage in the book of Job, which includes a particular reference to staying behind a safe door:

> Others try to hide their sins,
>   but I have never concealed mine.
> I have never feared what people would say;
>   I have never kept quiet or stayed indoors
>   because I feared their scorn.   (Job 31:32–4 GNT)

Now, can we say with Job that we have never remained silent, or stayed indoors, or out of the way to avoid meeting people, to avoid being challenged, put on the spot, for fear of what people may think or say about our response?

> Help us, Lord of all true wisdom, always to speak
> carefully, kindly, sincerely and truthfully.
> May we never be silent when a helpful or
> encouraging word is needed,
> and may we never speak thoughtlessly when
> silence would be better.
> We ask it in the Name of Him who always said

the right thing at the right time, but Who also
knew when to be silent,
Jesus Chriſt our Lord. Amen.

It is so important to get a right balance between times for silence and times for talk. We need our times of silence and solitude
when we can be still with God. A space to listen and reflect, a time
for quiet learning and renewal. As the psalmist says, 'For God
alone my soul waits in silence' (Ps. 62:1).

This expresses a deep longing to be alone and wait upon
God. How often we hear in the Gospels that Jesus withdrew to
a quiet place, a place where He could be alone with God, His
Father. This could be a place in the countryside, a room in a
friend's house, or up on a mountain:

> And after he had dismissed the crowds, he went up the
> mountain by himself to pray. When evening came, he was
> there alone.   (Matt. 14:23)

Jesus was following a long tradition in His culture of going apart
to pray and to find peace to hear God. The Prophet Isaiah re-
ferred to quietness being a strength:

> For thus said the Lord God, the Holy One of Israel:
> In returning and reſt you shall be saved;
> in quietness and in truſt shall be your ſtrength.   (Is. 30:15)

It is important to trust in quietness. *Silence is a virtue*, as the
saying goes. There is a very appropriate saying by the Desert
Father Abba Poemen in relation to keeping quiet; he does not
mince his words:

> It is not wooden doors we were taught to shut; the door we need
> to keep shut is the mouth.

Abba Poemen (*c.* 340–450)

> Set a guard over my mouth, O Lord; keep watch over the door
> of my lips.   (Ps. 141:3)

The door is, however, not only the door which is the mouth, the tool that utters noise; there is at the same time also the Door of Silence. Amidst all the clamour of life today, it becomes increasingly difficult for people to find a silent place. Through the Door of Silence we can enter and go in, and when we find a still place we shall there give thanks to God.

Ponder

Listen to the Silence.
Be still and let your soul catch up.

Scottish Proverb

THE DOOR OF SOLITUDE

> But whenever you pray, go into your room and shut the door
> and pray to your Father who is in secret; and your Father who
> sees in secret will reward you. (Matt. 6:6)

We all have to find time and space where we can be still and wait
upon God, listen and be led by the Holy Spirit. This may ask a
lot of us, but we know that it is God who will give us the
strength we need to do His work.

> It is by fastening the whole spirit of contemplation in ... silence
> and solitude ... set over and against the rich fellowship of the
> common life, that perfecting of balance, that adjustment be-
> tween the social and silent life that should make each rise and
> be ready and ripe to receive the Spiritual gifts that God may be
> pleased to give.
>
> Fr Lucius Cary SSJE (1866–1950)

Personal times of retreat are an important part of life: times to
withdraw from the many demands of the daily round to seek
and find refreshment and renewal. It is important to have a place
where we can relax and feel at home, and where we know we
can be alone and wait upon God.

> What was a closed door of mystery, prayer finds to be an open
> way to God.
>
> Fr George Congreve SSJE (1835–1918)

So, as you enter your inner room of prayer, with the door closed,
there you will not only intercede but also wait upon God in the
stillness and silence.

> Seek in reading and thou shalt find in meditation, knock in
> prayer and it shall be opened to thee in contemplation.
>
> St John of the Cross (1542–1591)

It is there for us to find, and it is our responsibility to seek it and, having found it, to use it. Our response, that free response of love, is to be still and quiet and concentrate our whole energy in contemplation as we learn to overcome the many things that can distract us.

> It is as the predominance of the Thou and the insignificance and self-importance of the Ego is more completely realised that the activity of the creature knocking on the door of the Divine Mystery is thrown back on the emptiness of its own self so that it should know that in and through its own self it can do nothing except to express and be that which God may give — even to the extent that its prayer is not its act but that which God may give. If that is so and it is the truth of contemplative prayer, it must affect and act through the whole of life — body, soul and spirit — the whole Being.
>
> Fr Gilbert Shaw (1886–1967)

In all of us there is something of Mary and something of Martha. The Mary part is that quiet reflective side, the one that we find when we step aside from all the busyness of life in order to be still and listen to God. From this contemplative side, the Mary aspect of creation, comes the desire for, the strength, to *do*, and the joy in the doing of those things that fill our days. This is the Martha part.

Enclosure has been an element of monastic life for centuries; lived out in different ways in different communities. It is a way of barring the outside world from disturbing us, just as the pillar of cloud in Exodus guarded the door of the tent so that none could enter and disturb Moses while he was speaking with the Lord:

> When Moses entered the tent, the pillar of cloud would descend and stand at the entrance of the tent, and the Lord would speak with Moses. (Ex. 33:9)

This sort of enclosure was part of the life of the prophets, but it was a temporary enclosure. Moses's servant, Joshua, expressed a more permanent withdrawal from the world, as he would not leave the tent at all:

> Thus the Lord used to speak to Moses face to face, as one speaks to a friend. Then he would return to the camp; but his young assistant, Joshua son of Nun, would not leave the tent.
>
> (Ex. 33:11)

There are communities that live a more enclosed life than others in order to be free from outside matters that could distract them from the life of prayer, contemplation and study to which God has called them.

The Covid-19 pandemic from 2020 put enclosure into a context for our times, when it affected nations, not just small groups. People were asked to stay at home, an enforced enclosure with no choice nor time to prepare; an enclosure that many found difficult and distressing. People could not go out, and could not enjoy the lightness of visiting others or of inviting guests in, to open the doors of friendship and hospitality. Nor could they find relief from the constant presence of those with whom they lived.

Other doors were opened, though: many found the experience liberating or transformative. Many found relief through our ability to communicate and see each other using the internet. A new form of ministry evolved in this medium, but in principle it was still the ministry of conversation between one and another. Everyone, including churches evolved new ways of working.

Life can be difficult when people are living in close quarters all the time. But from this demand can come a fresh and profound understanding of, and joy in, family life, or the corporate life of any group or community. God may be showing us more about ourselves and how He wants us to go forward as we learn to live with others. The enforced enclosure during the Covid-19 pandemic was for many a time of stress and tension, but for some it has also been an opportunity to draw closer to God in quiet moments and to discover that deep silence and joy when a physical enclosure becomes an enclosure of the heart. So, those of us who have survived this experience unharmed may rejoice, but we must remember in our rejoicing those who have been damaged by the Door of Enclosure slamming on them.

Ponder

A brother in Scetis went to ask for a word from Abba Moses and the old man said to him, 'Go and sit in your cell and your cell will teach you everything.'

From the *Apophthegmata Patrum* (*c.* 5th century)

THE DOOR OF SOLITARY & CONTEMPLATIVE PRAYER

> And whenever you pray, do not be like the hypocrites; for they love to stand and pray in the synagogues and at the street corners, so that they may be seen by others. Truly I tell you, they have received their reward. But whenever you pray, go into your room and shut the door and pray to your Father who is in secret; and your Father who sees in secret will reward you.
>
> (Matt. 6:5–6)

Is that not exactly what we are enjoined to do, day by day, when we spend time in prayer? How blest we are if we have a private room, perhaps a special place which is ours, our private place where we can be alone with God. We sometimes forget just what a privilege it is to have access to our own space, where we can go and close the door behind us and know that we can be alone and undisturbed. Let us be very thankful for this, something many, many people long for, but cannot have.

If we have this place, we have a duty to make good use of it. There are so many subjects for prayer, as we all know from reading the papers or listening to the news. It is our faithfulness in bringing these things to God that matters, however inadequate we may feel. What matters is giving this time our energy, our whole selves. We should remember in our prayers those who do not have the blessing of time and space to pray, and who long for it.

> [Prayer] is not separate from the rest of life. We do want to watch that the Spirit does develop our prayer ... Yet we have to recognize that just waiting is an important part of prayer. Waiting upon God avoids the state of inertia or self-hypnotism.
>
> Fr Gilbert Shaw (1886–1967)

The silent way of prayer that we call contemplative prayer is God's gift to us. We stop using words, reciting prayers, *asking* for things, and listen in silence for God, and within that silence God opens doors to us—indeed the prayer itself is a Door that opens to us new vistas, gives us new ideas, shows us when God wants us to work for Him.

> There is in true contemplation an urgency to love God for himself, and also a desire that all should be drawn to respond to this mercy, and accept the reconciliation accomplished by, with, and in Christ.
>
> 'Reconciliation' from the SLG Oblate Rule

Contemplative prayer, whether on retreat, at home or anywhere else, is the key that opens different and sometimes difficult doors for us at different times in our lives.

In our prayer we say, *By your power help me to fulfil my good resolves.* However much you are involved in the ministry of service to others, there is always that return to the quiet waiting upon God. The Martha and Mary aspects are in us all, with the one being more dominant than the other at various stages in life. So we need to wait in our place of solitude in a state of alertness, not drifting into somnolence or allowing our thoughts to wander. This can be hard and it can be demoralizing:

> I throw myself down in my chamber, and I call in, and invite God, and all his Angels thither, and when they are there, I neglect God and his angels for the noise of a fly, the rattling of a coach, for the whining of a door.
>
> John Donne (1572–1631)

Is that not true? Does it not resonate with us all in some way? Yet when we are recollected and abandoned to God, the very walls could fall down around us and not disturb us. If we persevere and work at solitary prayer, it can bring great rewards, and can open a door that perhaps we do not even know is there.

> Through a year of hard mental discipline, carried on with homely unseen heroism, she learned to silence the chatter of self, to focus her mind in meditation, until the beauty dwelt upon became not

a picture, but an opening door, and then with sealed lips but open ears to go through it by her secret stair to God.

Elizabeth Goudge (1900–1984)

We probably all have our own particular way, or secret stair to God. It matters less what the way is than that we follow it and wait upon God in contemplation. Let us always remember that this is a gift from God and give thanks for it.

O name of Jesus, key to all gifts,
Open up for me the great door to your treasure house.
So may I enter and praise you
with the praise that comes from the heart.
I return for your mercies
which I have experienced in latter days,
for you came and rescued me
with an awareness of a New World.
May such awareness be ours too. Amen.

Isaac of Nineveh (c. 613–c. 700)

Ponder

But the silence in the mind
is when we live best, within
listening distance of the silence
we call God.

R. S. Thomas (1913–2000)

THE DOOR OF OPPORTUNITY

> And he was afraid, and said, "How awesome is this place! This is none other than the house of God, and this is the gate of heaven." (Gen. 28:17)

This exclamation of amazement was made by Jacob, who had found God in a special way—"How awesome is this place!" Yes, how holy, how full of God. So full of God that Jacob calls it the 'house of God', the 'gate of heaven'.

Sometimes we have these awesome moments when we know that God is very near. He is near always, but we are not always aware or awake to His presence. Such moments give us an opportunity to open the door of our heart and let God in—and let Love embrace us, and we others.

These special moments are an opportunity to gain self-knowledge, to spend time being with oneself and with God; finding the gate of heaven here in the awesomeness of the ordinary. But every moment is an opportunity to be open and ready to receive all that God wants to give us as we continue our search for faith and conversion, that we may become His people as He would have us be.

> Conversion is the process in which we are given opportunity upon opportunity to accept the free gift of salvation.
>
> Macrina Wiederkehr (1939–2020)

The door of opportunity opens both inward and out. Let us open that door and go through remembering that Jesus said, 'I am the Door', and 'I am the Way.' We are not expected to act in our own faith but in God-given strength, if we have faith to accept it. Any conversion or act of renewal that involves a change in the way we express our Christianity is an act of faith, as it is written in the Acts of the Apostles. God will open the Door of Opportunity to us if only we ask.

Ponder

When they arrived, they called the church together and related all that God had done with them, and how he had opened a door of faith for the Gentiles. (Acts 14:27)

THE DOOR OF JOY

The secret of joy in work is contained in one word—
EXCELLENCE. To know how to do something well is to
enjoy it.

Pearl S. Buck (1892–1973)

> Supposedly the gardener
> He rose early,
> the fresh earth
> sweet to His sense,
> and under the apple trees
> the daffodils in bud.
>
> Supposing Him
> the gardener,
> laughter returned to us
> at morning,
> seeing His glory
> at the sun's rising.

Anon.

When he knocked at the outer gate, a maid named Rhoda came
to answer. On recognizing Peter's voice, she was so overjoyed
that, instead of opening the gate, she ran in and announced that
Peter was standing at the gate. (Acts 12:13–14)

Why was Rhoda so overjoyed that she could not open the door,
but ran for help? Because the last they knew of Peter was that
he was in prison. Now here he is knocking at the door and asking to come in. We know that Peter had been miraculously
released from prison by angels, but those in that house did not,
and so were fearful. However, Peter's persistent knocking made
them open the door and admit him to hear his astonishing story
with great joy.

What is joy? Happiness, gladness, exaltation of spirit … One image I like is that it is 'sunshine of the mind'. We so often see only the downside of life and fail to rejoice over the good. Do we see the problems of our life and forget to rejoice with thanksgiving for all its benefits?

So what about joy: what opens the Door of Joy to you, to me? What makes your heart sing for joy, gives you sunshine of mind? God is all the beauty and splendour of nature, the spontaneity of children's laughter, moments in the liturgy when some words in the Psalms or readings lift the heart in a special way. Do we share these moments? We can both give and gain encouragement by sharing, as those early Christians shared their joy. Throughout the Bible we read of joy and rejoicing as well as sadness and war, as in the following passages:

> They offered great sacrifices that day and rejoiced, for God had made them rejoice with great joy; the women and children also rejoiced. The joy of Jerusalem was heard far away.
>
> (Neh. 12:43)

> You show me the path of life. In your presence there is fullness of joy; in your right hand are pleasures for evermore.
>
> (Ps. 16:11)

> By contrast, the fruit of the Spirit is love, joy, peace, patience, kindness, generosity, faithfulness, gentleness, and self-control. There is no law against such things.   (Gal. 5:22)

In her writing about the life of St Seraphim of Sarov, Valentine Zander says:

> As for the joy of Easter, he relived it every day, constantly singing the hymn of the Resurrection. Thus far away Palestine came very near and he lived at Jesus' feet as though in the Holy Lands watching in the interior Jerusalem of the heart, ceaselessly keeping the name of Jesus on his lips.
>
> Valentine Zander

So we too must try to keep the Door of Joy open and to present ourselves cheerful in our approach to life. In this way we shall be the kind of witnesses to the faith that we profess, so that others will want to follow.

Ponder

Eternal life consists in the joyful society of all the Blessed. What makes this society a supremely delightful one is the fact that each and every one of its members will share equally all they have. Each loves the others as he loves himself and is as happy about another's well-being as if it were his own. And so the greater the happiness of any one member, the greater the happiness of all.

St Thomas Aquinas (1225–1274)

THE DOOR OF FREEDOM

Since the Son hath made me free,
Let me taste my liberty;
Thee behold with open face,
Triumph in thy saving grace,
Thy great will delight to prove,
Glory in thy perfect love.

Charles Wesley (1707–1788)

Now the Lord is the Spirit, and where the Spirit of the Lord is, there is freedom. (2 Cor. 3:17)

For freedom Christ has set us free. Stand firm, therefore, and do not submit again to a yoke of slavery. (Gal. 5:1)

Look, I have set before you an open door, which no one is able to shut. (Rev. 3:8)

These quotations from the New Testament tell us there is freedom. We can be free. The door is open. Why then are we so often tense, enslaved by boundaries of our own making, our own fears and prejudices? By things we cannot, or will not, or do not let go and release to God?

> Therefore, the simplest definition of freedom is this: it means the ability to do the will of God. To be able to resist His will is not to be free. In sin there is no freedom.
>
> Thomas Merton (1915–1968)

We may be afraid of where the Door of Freedom will lead, of the demands it will make on our way of life; how it will take us out of the rut we are in, because in our blindness we cannot see beyond, to the fullness of life this will bring and the freedom we gain. We lack the faith, the trust.

> Faith renders us open to the power of God. Accordingly it is the liberation of our most intimate self, the redemption of our heart. It is as if God pulls aside a bolt in our deepest self and a door opens. Through this opening he can flow through into the deepest dimensions of our self and pull it along in the loving grip and restorative power of his omnipotence.
>
> André Louf (1929–2010)

Life is full of constraints of one sort or another. These may restrict our freedom of choice and can be frustrating too, but the freedom of inner self is another matter. In *New Wine Skins*, Sandra Schneiders writes:

> It is as true today as it has ever been that true freedom is to be found in union with the will of God. The only solid ground of obedience is freedom, and genuine Christian freedom cannot be bestowed on us by law, structures or superiors. Freedom is the gift of God to the person who has given up on the law as justification and given himself or herself up to the infinitely merciful God who is the Father of Jesus Christ.
>
> Sandra M. Schneiders

In the Benedictus, the canticle for Morning Prayer, the word 'free' occurs three times:

Blessed be the Lord the God of Israel, who has come to his people and set them free ... to set us free from the hands of our enemies, free to worship him without fear, ...

Common Worship

The mere ability to choose between good and evil is the most basic form of freedom. Perfect spiritual freedom is a total ability to make an evil choice. Freedom, therefore, does not consist in an equal balance between good and evil choices, but in the perfect love and acceptance of what is really good and the perfect hatred and rejection of what is evil, so that everything you do is good and makes you happy, and you refuse and deny and ignore every possibility that might lead to unhappiness, self-deception and grief. Only the person who has rejected all evil so completely that they are unable to desire it at all is truly free.

Liberty, then, is a talent given us by God, an instrument to work with. It is the tool with which we build our lives, our happiness. Our true liberty is something we must never sacrifice, for if we sacrifice it we renounce God himself. It is our liberty that makes us persons, constituted in the Divine Image.

Much rests with us: do we want to be free? Are we willing to let go and let God open our hearts to receive His gift of freedom? It may mean a desert experience, a time of darkness, a time of deep searching in order to come to the place where we can let go and break out of the chains that enslave us, with thanksgiving.

Ponder

Were you a slave when called? Do not be concerned about it. Even if you can gain your freedom, make use of your present condition now more than ever. For whoever was called in the Lord as a slave is a freed person belonging to the Lord, just as whoever was free when called is a slave of Christ.

(1 Cor. 7:21–2)

THE DOOR OF FRIENDSHIP

A friend is one who knows who you are,
Understands where you have been,
Accepts who you've become,
And still gently invites you to grow.

Anon.

A good deed is never lost; he who sows courtesy reaps
friendship, and he who plants kindness gathers love.

St Basil (330–379)

A friend loves at all times.   (Prov. 17:17)

We surely all have friends, or more probably a particular friend, with whom we like to share our joys, and sorrows; by whom we can be understood and comforted. However much or little we see of those people, when we do meet that connection opens — or re-opens — a door that is otherwise closed, and we pick up the threads as if we had never been apart.

Friends are the sunshine of life.

John Hay (1838–1905)

That saying probably sums up our experiences of deep, true and lasting friendships. A friend is one who knows who you are, understands where you have been, accepts who you have become and gently invites you grow. Such a friend is like an open door, always open to let us enter.

Some friendships do not last, but some friends are more loyal than brothers or sisters. This is what is expressed in the second half of the verse from Proverbs that I gave above:

A friend loves at all times,
and kinsfolk are born to share adversity.   (Prov. 17:17)

Ælred of Rievaulx wrote about both spiritual friendship and the everyday relationships with friends:

> Spiritual friendship should be desired not for consideration of any worldly advantage, or for any extrinsic cause, but for the dignity of its own nature and the feelings of the human heart, so that its fruition and reward is nothing other than itself.
>
> ...
>
> There are four qualities that must be tested in a friend, so that you may trust yourself to this friend securely: loyalty, right intention, discretion and patience ... However, there is nothing more praiseworthy in friendship than loyalty, which seems to be its nurse and guardian.
>
> Ælred of Rievaulx (1110–1167)

Friendship here sounds like a difficult task, almost a challenge. But it is also an immense privilege. Jesus explained friendship in a dramatic way:

> No one has greater love than this, to lay down one's life for one's friends. You are my friends if you do what I command you. I do not call you servants any longer, because the servant does not know what the master is doing; but I have called you friends, because I have made known to you everything that I have heard from my Father. (John 15:13–15)

He makes it clear that the demands of friendship can be very great indeed. It may seem difficult to enter this Door of Friendship, but once we have gone through we can reap its benefits.

Ponder

One who forgives an affront fosters friendship,
but one who dwells on disputes will alienate a friend.

(Prov. 17:9)

THE DOOR OF HOSPITALITY

Listen! I am standing at the door, knocking; if you hear my voice and open the door, I will come in to you and eat with you, and you with me.   (Rev. 3:20)

It is our Lord Jesus who knocks on the door, and we shall open it. We shall open it and show Him our full hospitality.

To welcome is one of the signs of true human and Christian maturity. It is not only to open one's home to someone. It is to give space to someone in one's heart, space for that person to be and to grow; space where the person knows that he or she is accepted just as they are, with their wounds and their gifts.

Jean Vanier (1928–2019)

The Door of Hospitality is present in some sense in most other ministries. Hospitality involves giving and receiving friendship, coupled with listening.

Do not neglect to show hospitality to strangers, for by doing that some have entertained angels without knowing it.

(Heb. 13:2)

It is not only about a chat over a cup of tea or coffee, is it? It is much more than that—the welcoming smile, the having time for a person or persons without being on edge because we are thinking about the next thing we have to do. It is opening one's heart in love as one meets people.

Remember the presence of God and His indwelling in any to whom we may be speaking.

SLG Rule

Our experience of restrictions on movement and gathering together to protect others from disease during the Covid-19 pandemic has highlighted how important hospitality is in our lives, and how its lack can leave us bereft and anxious. However, when we cannot invite people into our homes and our lives, this leaves a space to invite God in, and this in turn reminds us that whenever we invite someone into our homes, we also invite God.

Ponder

Truly I tell you, just as you did it to one of the least of these brothers and sisters of mine, you did it to me.   (Matt. 25:40)

THE DOOR OF UTTERANCE

> At the same time pray for us as well that God will open to us
> a door for the word, that we may declare the mystery of
> Christ, for which I am in prison, so that I may reveal it clearly,
> as I should. (Col. 4:3–4)

A 'door for the word'—or a 'door of utterance', as the King
James Version translates it—that is a door to speaking of the
mystery of Christ. Although utterance is an old-fashioned
word, one we do not use much today, yet it seems the right expression here. There are times when we simply long for the
right word, for the Door of Utterance to open to us, so that we
can say the right thing in a difficult situation, or when writing
a letter, or simply in day-to-day living. We have only to trust,
to have faith that God will give us the words to speak, to
preach, to write.

There are, of course, moments of knowledge, discernment,
enlightenment; moments of joy when the words simply flow. For
such times let us be truly thankful, just as the disciples must have
been when they preached the Word and were inspired by God
in what they said:

> When I came to Troas to proclaim the good news of Christ, a
> door was opened for me in the Lord. (2 Cor. 2:12)

Equally, there are times when the knowledge of the word is
there but we do not want to know. Why? Perhaps because it is
too difficult, too painful, or we turn a deaf ear, or a blind eye,
and miss an opportunity of witnessing to our faith. We let God
down. Do we not need the forthrightness of those early
Christians to speak or write of the Love of God? If we are to be
true to our vocation, that is to our dedication to the Love of God,
surely we must endeavour to be alive to the opportunities that

come our way: God-given moments providing us with the opportunity to be a witness to our faith, to speak of the mystery of God, praying always for a deeply prayerful utterance.

For those who work in counselling, or who give spiritual direction, knowing what to say and when must be of prime importance—and how Christians must value the gift of discernment! So we pray that God will open to us the Door of Utterance.

Be not anxious. Do not worry: if we are to be ready and available to do God's work, we must be prepared to spend time quietly before God, waiting and listening, spending time with the Bible or another spiritual text in meditation, trusting in God to open the Door of Utterance for us.

Ponder

Do not worry about how you are to speak
or what you are to say, for what you are to
say will be given you at the time. (Matt. 10.19)

THE DOOR OF WATCHING & WAITING

In stillness nailed
To hold all time,
all change,
all circumstance in and to
Love's embrace.

Anonymous English nun

Happy is the one who listens to me, watching daily at my
gates, waiting beside my doors. (Prov. 8:34)

This text from Proverbs conveys a message of hope to those who
watch and wait upon the Lord. Blessed is the one who hears
God's call and listens to His word, steadfast in watching and
waiting upon the Lord, ever ready to do His will, whatever that
may be. To stand ready, however difficult or unwelcome it may
be, however much sorrow or joy it may involve, simply ready
and waiting to be used.

Be like those who are waiting for their master to return from
the wedding banquet, so that they may open the door for him
as soon as he comes and knocks. (Luke 12:36)

This should be our constant prayer: *Lord, make us willing to
be willing to do all you ask of us*. Quietly waiting and watching in
prayer and contemplation at all times, abandoned to God in
whom is perfect freedom.

Consider the Old Testament leaders, how they must have
waited and watched before God in the Temple, in the fields
while tending their flocks, or following the plough. They must
have sometimes thought of God as great and terrible, awesome,
but also as a friend, one who could be trusted to help them in
their troubles.

There are times in the church year when we are particularly called to watch, to wait, to wonder: Advent and Lent, and especially Holy Week. In Advent we are watching and waiting for the coming of our Lord at Christmas, the birth of Jesus our Saviour. In Lent we watch and wait with the Lord as we prepare to go with Him through His passion, death and resurrection. What was it like for our Lord in that first Holy Week, watching, waiting, wondering? What is it like for Jesus today? How He watches and waits for us to claim all the gifts He has for us, freely given in love, by love.

We are especially watchful during Lent: watchful in many areas of our lives, particularly our prayer time, our Bible Study and meditations on the Holy Scriptures; our relationships with one another, our families and friends, and with God. We also consider our food and fasting, our use of time and leisure.

How tremendous are the gifts of our faith, surely worth any amount of watching and waiting! In both Advent and Lent there is a degree of expectation and hope, for we are fortunate that we know all will be well in the end. How we rejoice at Christmas for the long-awaited Saviour, or at Easter for our risen Lord. But as Christians, we also watch and wait each day of our lives for the coming of the Lord, always ready.

Ponder

Keep awake therefore, for you do not know on what day your Lord is coming. But understand this: if the owner of the house had known in what part of the night the thief was coming, he would have stayed awake and would not have let his house be broken into. Therefore you also must be ready, for the Son of Man is coming at an unexpected hour.   (Matt. 24:42–4)

THE DOOR OF LISTENING

O that my people would listen to me,
that Israel would walk in my ways!   (Ps. 81:13)

Is that not what God must be saying in the here and now of the twenty-first century, again and again? O that my people would listen to me, instead of rushing about doing this and that; only sometimes stopping to pray, to implore me to do the things that they think are the answer to their, or their friends', or indeed to the world's problems.

> Some one came knocking
> At my wee, small door;
> Someone came knocking;
> I'm sure—sure—sure;
> I listened, I opened,
> I looked to left and right,
> But nought there was a stirring
> In the still dark night;
> Only the busy beetle
> Tap-tapping in the wall,
> Only from the forest
> The screech-owl's call,
> Only the cricket whistling
> While the dewdrops fall,
> So I know not who came knocking,
> At all, at all, at all.
>
> Walter de la Mare, 'Some One' (1873–1956)

My sheep hear my voice. I know them, and they follow me.
                                                (John 10:27–8)

In my village infant school I memorized all sorts of things, but one verse has stayed with me particularly:

The wise old owl sat in an oak,
The more he saw, the less he spoke,
The less he spoke, the more he heard,
Let's emulate that wise old bird.

So often we hear things, read things, but have not really heard because we have not truly *listened*; that is, listened at a deep level with uncluttered minds. We cannot hope to understand anything that the Lord may be trying to show us, tell us, or give us, if we are only listening with half an ear, the other half being concerned with what to have for dinner, or the weather, our work, or any of a host of other things.

> But this command I gave them, 'Obey my voice, and I will be your God, and you shall be my people; and walk only in the way that I command you, so that it may be well with you.' Yet they did not obey or incline their ear, but, in the stubbornness of their evil will, they walked in their own counsels, and looked backwards rather than forwards. (Jer. 7:23–4)

That resonates with me. How often we can miss the point by not paying attention, by not inclining the ear, not really *listening*, but allowing our thoughts to wander—then realizing, *Oh, I missed that, I've lost the thread!* In this sense, then, *listening* is the way; and it is a door. If we go through the Door of Listening, then we enter onto the right way, to follow the way that God has marked out for us.

> The Lord tells us the first task in life is this: prayer. But not the prayer of words, like a parrot, but prayer of the heart; gazing on the Lord, hearing the Lord.
>
> Pope Francis

By calling for attentive listening to the word of God I seek to stress the primacy of listening to God's Word. We need to give time to this question of listening with our whole being. If we hear but have not really listened, we don't get the message. It takes time to be still and quiet, with hearts open ready to hear and listen, to listen in a deep place of inner silence. Be still, oh my soul. Be still and *listen*.

Ponder

Be still, my soul; the Lord is on your side;
bear patiently the cross of grief or pain;
leave to your God to order and provide;
in ev'ry change He faithful will remain.
Be still, my soul; your best, your heav'nly friend
through thorny ways leads to a joyful end.

Be still, my soul; your God will undertake
to guide the future as He has the past;
your hope, your confidence, let nothing shake;
all now mysterious shall be bright at last.
Be still, my soul; the waves and winds still know
His voice who ruled them while He lived below.

Be still, my soul; when dearest friends depart
and all is darkened in the vale of tears,
then you will better know His love, His heart,
who comes to soothe your sorrows and your fears.
Be still, my soul; your Jesus can repay
from His own fullness all He takes away.

Be still, my soul; the hour is hast'ning on
when we shall be forever with the Lord,
when disappointment, grief, and fear are gone,
sorrow forgot, love's purest joys restored.
Be still my soul; when change and tears are past,
all safe and blessed we shall meet at last.

Katharina von Schlegel (1697–after 1768),
trans. Jane Borthwick (1813–1897)

DOORS OPENED BY TEARS

Again I saw all the oppressions that are practised under the
sun. Look, the tears of the oppressed—with no one to comfort
them! On the side of their oppressors there was power—with
no one to comfort them. (Eccl. 4:1)

For I wrote to you out of much distress and anguish of heart
and with many tears, not to cause you pain, but to let you
know the abundant love that I have for you. (2 Cor. 2:4)

When we start to think about the doors that tears can open, what
are we seeking? Are we looking for quick answers to problems,
or for self-knowledge or comfort, or are we risking surprise, dis-
illusionment, or misunderstanding, and hurt?

We know that tears can open many doors—those of grief,
compassion, anger, guilt, sorrow, joy, prayer and love; but do
we want to know? Would we not rather sail along on a calm
sea than be tossed by storm waves? After all, tears can be an
embarrassment: they can need explaining, but they can also
bring relief, healing, friendship; and for some people tears are
a safety valve.

Before all else, pray to be given tears, that weeping may soften
the savage hardness which is in your soul and, having acknowl-
edged your sins unto the Lord, you may receive from Him the
remission of sins.

Evagrius Ponticus (*c*. 346–399)

The tears that Evagrius describes are clearly something very
positive. Isaac of Nineveh is considered to be the great teacher
of the Doctrine of Tears. He described the gift as a sign of new
birth that comes after a long period of purification.

So long as you have not reached the realm of tears, that which
is hidden within you serves the world—that is, you still lead a

worldly life and do the work of God only with your outer man, while the inner man is barren; for his fruit begins with tears.

Isaac of Nineveh (*c.* 613–*c.* 700)

So, why should we not let the tears flow and let God teach us through them? This He surely will, if we are open and ready to listen and receive, and to count tears a gift. St Teresa of Ávila talked of the Gift of Tears, and she mentions tears many times in her writings:

The Desert Fathers, in fact, constantly exhorted their followers to pray for the gift of compunction, the gift of tears. These Fathers felt that when the soul was softened by this interior weeping, God would give the experience of his light; in the shadow of sorrow was to be found the spiritual joy of enlightenment.

Teresa of Ávila (1515–1582)

Others, such as Pope Gregory the Great, also speak of the need to pray for the Gift of Tears:

Who does good works and has been deemed worthy to have received some gifts from God, but has not yet received tears, he must pray for this in order to weep, either thinking about the last judgment or longing for the heavenly kingdom or repenting over evil past deeds or kneeling before the Cross of Christ, seeing Him suffering for us, our Crucified Saviour.

Pope Gregory I (*c.* 540–604)

These tears are a gift to us in the sense that they improve us, they ultimately bring us joy.

There are tears that arise from sorrow and there are tears that arise from joy, just as our Lord said: you shall weep, lament and sorrow, but the world will rejoice; but often a time when your tears will be turned to joy.

Anonymous Syriac Father

Tears can be a gift when they cleanse us. Some people may weep because of their sins—and if that is the case, they do well to do so.

Sorrow that is because of God is compunction which turns one to salvation. Others may have moved away from sinful acts to perform good deeds: they weep in joy, out of love for their Lord who has performed a great act of grace for them, delivering them from the slavery of death, and making them free; for these people have humbled themselves and kept his commandments.

from *The Syriac Book of Steps* (c. 400)

Simeon the New Theologian writes movingly of tears as cleansing the stains of his soul and the darkness of his mind to make him light enough to see God. However, during prayer we need to be careful not to induce tears just for the sake of weeping; such tears will not help towards purification of the soul, but rather hinder us.

The tears that come unbidden, when we least expect them, are often brushed away—a nuisance—this is not the moment for weeping. Yet if we can stay with them, then the doors can be opened and the Spirit teach us through them. It may be through these tears that a door of friendship is opened and we see our need to be a friend to someone whose needs we have not been fully aware of until that moment. Perhaps we are being shown our own lack of friendliness. Isaac of Nineveh has left us this prayer, in which he thanks God for the gift of tears:

I beseech You, O God,
send me help from your highest heavens
so that I may keep afar from my heart
every evil intention and every carnal wish.
Do not cast me, Lord, from your protection
lest my adversary find me
and trample upon me just as he desires,
destroying me utterly.
It is You who grants repentance and a sorrowing heart
to the sinner who repents;
in this way
you ease his heart of the weight of sin

that is laid upon it,
thanks to the comfort which comes from sorrowing
and from the gift of tears.

Isaac of Nineveh (*c*. 613–*c*. 700)

Ponder

Tears give the mind a greater knowledge of God and oneself.

Isaac of Nineveh

DEATH, THE DOOR TO HEAVEN

After this I looked, and there in heaven a door stood open!
(Rev. 4:1)

So often death is thought of as the end and, yes, it is the end of life on earth, but it is also the way to heaven, to life eternal.

> Human death is a door through which we all are, both consciously and unconsciously, gathered up for judgement and for perfection. Body, soul and spirit are one unity, created for one purpose to be all for God. The physical is not held by death as our Lord makes absolutely clear and certain, 'I am the resurrection and the life' — that is the good news of the Church. Through the divine mercy presented in life we are taken by the grace of God into Christ's eternal life which is the first fruits of the dead. Death had no hold on Him.
>
> Fr Gilbert Shaw (1886–1967)

The 1979 American Book of Common Prayer includes the following text to be read at the service for the burial of an adult:

> O God, who by the glorious resurrection of your son Jesus Christ destroyed death, and brought life and immortality to light: Grant that your servant N., being raised with him, may know the strength of his presence, and rejoice in his eternal glory; who with you and the Holy Spirit lives and reigns, one God, for ever and ever. Amen.
>
> *Book of Common Prayer,* use of the Episcopal Church

Death is not the end. Rather, death is a door, a door opened to us by Jesus Christ. It is a door to go through to a new life, a life with, and in, Christ. It is not a door that we should fear, but one that we should welcome because it will bring us, finally and completely, into the pure love of God.

Ponder

Soon after you're dead—we're not sure how long, but not long—
you'll be united with the most ecstatic love you've ever known.
As one of the best things in your life was human love, this will
be love, but much more satisfying, and it will last forever.

Cardinal Basil Hume (1923–1999)

THE CONCEALED DOOR: HOLINESS

Blessed are the pure in heart, for they will see God.

(Matt. 5:8)

Through the ages there have been people called by God for special work, to spread the good news of the Gospel. We venerate them as saints throughout the liturgical year. These were people set apart for particular work for God. When Jesus called His first disciples they were not from the nobility or the educated classes, they were simple folk, as were many of those who came in the centuries to follow.

Some, through their faith and love for God, have gathered followers and the nucleus of a religious community has been formed and grown, to spread eventually throughout the world: St Benedict, St Francis, St Bernard, St Bruno, St Teresa, and many others. These people of prayer and love of God gave their lives to this work, not always with much encouragement and often in the face of opposition. Despite all their difficulties they opened a concealed door to their hearts and allowed the gifts and talents God had given them to be used to His glory.

Our talents are the gift that God gives to us ... What we make of our talents is our gift back to God.

Leo Buscaglia

Unless a person opens that hidden, concealed door of the heart, these talents cannot be released and used for God's good purposes. We all have some gifts or talents which can and should be used for the glory of God. The key to that door is prayer. So let us keep faithful in prayer, the key that unlocks concealed doors.

Ponder

O Thou who camest from above,
the pure celestial fire to impart
kindle a flame of sacred love
upon the mean altar of my heart.

There let it for thy glory burn
with inextinguishable blaze,
and trembling to its source return,
in humble prayer and fervent praise.

Jesus, confirm my heart's desire
to work and speak and think for thee;
still let me guard the holy fire,
and still stir up thy gift in me.

Ready for all thy perfect will,
my acts of faith and love repeat,
till death thy endless mercies seal,
and make my sacrifice complete.

Charles Wesley (1707–1788)

So I say to you,
Ask, and it will be
given you; search,
and you will find;
knock, and the
door will be
opened for you.
For everyone who
asks receives,
and everyone who
searches finds,
and for everyone
who knocks, the
door will be
opened.

(Luke 11:9–10)

SOURCES OF QUOTATIONS

Ambrose of Milan, *Sermon 22, An Exposition of Psalm 118*, trans. in *Homilies of Saint Ambrose on Psalm 118 (119)*, trans. Í. M. Di Riain (Dublin: Halcyon Press, 1998), 43.

Ælred of Rievaulx, *On Spiritual Friendship*, trans. by Lawrence C. Braceland, ed. by Marsha L. Dutton, Cistercian Fathers 5 (Liturgical Press, 2010), Book I, paras 45–6, Book III, paras 61–2.

Story of Abba Antony, in *The Desert of the Heart: Daily Readings with the Desert Fathers*, introd. and ed. Sr Benedicta Ward SLG (SLG Press, 2016, 2nd edn 2022), 14.

Augustine, *Enarrationes in Psalmos*, 4.8, in Paul A. Böer Sr., ed., *St. Augustine on the Psalms*, 2 vols. (Christian Literature Publishing Co., 1886; facsimile in 1 vol., Martino Fine Books, 2012).

Brother Victor-Antoine d'Avila-Latourrette OSB, *Blessings of the Daily: A Monastic Book of Days* (Liguori Publications, 2002).

Anthony Bloom, *Living Prayer* (Templegate, 1966).

Paul A. Böer Sr., ed., *St. Augustine on the Psalms*, 2 vols. (Christian Literature Publishing Co., 1886; facsimile in 1 vol., Martino Fine Books, 2012).

The Book of Common Prayer [...] *According to the use of The Episcopal Church* (Church Publishing Incorporated, 2007).

The Book of Steps, Discourse XVIII: 'On the Tears of Prayer', cited in Sebastian P. Brock, *The Syriac Fathers on Prayer and the Spiritual Life* (Cistercian Publications, 1987).

Corrie ten Boom, *Clippings from My Notebook* (Thorndike Press, 1983).

Cynthia Bourgeault, *The Wisdom Jesus. Transforming Heart and Mind: A New Perspective on Christ and His Message* (Shambhala, 2008).

Sebastian P. Brock, *The Luminous Eye: The Spiritual World Vision of Saint Ephrem* (Cistercian Publications, 1992).

———, ed. and trans., *The Syriac Fathers on Prayer and the Spiritual Life* (Cistercian Publications, 1987).

Charles Capps, *Releasing the Ability of God Through Prayer* (Harrison House, 1978).

Bishop George Carey, *Sharing a Vision* (Darton, Longman & Todd, 1993).

Fr Lucius Cary SSJE, *Dicit on the SLG Rule*, unpublished typescript, 1929.

Fr George Congreve, *Christian Life: A Response with Other Retreat Addresses and Sermons* (Longmans, 1904).

Emily Dickinson, *The Complete Poems* (Faber & Faber, 2016), Poem 1619.

John Donne, *LXXX Sermons* (1640), 12 December 1626, 'At the Funeral of Sir William Cokayne'.

Evagrius Ponticus, *De Oratione*, in C. J. De Catanzaro, trans., *Saint Symeon (the New Theologian): The Discourses* (Paulist Press, 1980).

Lionel Fanthorpe, *Thoughts and Prayers* Series, 11 vols (Wordcatcher Publishing, 1995–2019).

Elizabeth Goudge, *Green Dolphin Country* (Hodder & Stoughton, 1944).

Prosper Guéranger, Cécile Bruyère, Paul Delatte, *The Spirit of Solesmes* (Burns & Oates, 1997).

Dag Hammarskjöld, 'A Room of Quiet (The United Nations Meditation Room)', in *Public Papers of the Secretaries-General of the United Nations*, vol. 3: *Dag Hammarskjöld, 1956–1957*, ed. Andrew W. Cordier and Wilder Foote (Columbia University Press, 1973), 710–11.

Urban T. Holmes III, *A History of Christian Spirituality: An Analytical Introduction* (Church Publishing Incorporated, 2002).

Basil Hume, *Cardinal Hume: In My Own Words* (Hodder & Stoughton, 1999).

Isaac of Nineveh, 'Discourse LXXIV', in Sebastian P. Brock, *The Syriac Fathers on Prayer and the Spiritual Life* (Cistercian Publications, 1987), 250 and 341.

——, *Homily 28, The Second Part*, Ch. 5, prayer 3, in Sebastian P. Brock, trans., *Isaac of Nineveh (Isaac the Syrian): 'the second part', chapters IV-XLI [Versio]*, 2 vols, Corpus Scriptorum Christianorum Orientalium 555/Scriptores Syri 225 (Peeters, 1995), vol. 2.

John of Apamea, *Letter to Hesychius,* paras 60, 61, 64, trans. in Sebastian P. Brock, *The Syriac Fathers on Prayer and the Spiritual Life* (Cistercian Publications, 1987), 81–98.

John of Dalyatha, Prayer in Letter 42:1, trans. in Mary Hansbury, *The Letters of John of Dalyatha* (Gorgias Press, 2006).

Kieran Kavanaugh, ed., *Collected Works of St. John of the Cross* (Institute of Carmelite Studies, 1973).

David A. Lichter, 'Tears and Contemplation in Isaac of Nineveh', *Diakonia* 11 (1976), 239–258.

André Louf, *Teach Us to Pray: Learning a Little about God,* trans. Robert Hoskins (Darton, Longman and Todd, 1974).

——, *Tuning in to Grace: The Quest for God*, trans. John Vriend (Liturgical Press, 1992).

George A. Maloney SJ, *Inward Stillness* (Dimension Books, 1981).

——, *Russian Hesychasm: The Spirituality of Nil Sorskij*, Slavistic Printings and Reprintings 269 (Mouton, 1973).

Thomas Merton, *Seeds of Contemplation* (New Directions, 1949).

Toki Miyashina: *This poem is reproduced widely in slightly varying translations, sometimes ascribed to 'Toki Miyashiro'. It has not been possible to find an original source or the name of a translator. The version reproduced here comes from* https://chandralynn.files.wordpress.com/2017/11/japanese-psalm-23-roses-arc.pdf (accessed 13 Jan 2023).

Dom Placid Murray OSB, *Commentary of Saint Ambrose on Psalm 118* (Halcyon Press, 1998).

Francis Kelly Nemeck OMI and Marie Theresa Coombs, *Called by God: A Theology of Vocation and Lifelong Commitment* (Wipf and Stock, 2001).

John Henry Parker, trans., *The Homilies of Saint John Chrysostom, Archbishop of Constantinople* (J. H. Parker, 1843, repr. Hansebooks, 2018).

Michael Perham, *Lively Sacrifice: The Eucharist in the Church of England Today* (SPCK, 1992).

John Pritchard, *The Life and Work of a Priest* (SPCK, 2007).

Joseph Roux, *Thoughts: Meditations of a Parish Priest*, with an introduction by Paul Mariéton, trans. from 3rd French edn by Isabel F. Hapgood (Thomas Y. Crowell & Co., 1886), 197 (no. lxv).

Sandra M. Schneiders, *New Wine Skins: Re-imagining Religious Life Today* (Paulist Press, 1986).

Gilbert Shaw, *Death: The Gateway to Life*, Fairacres Publications 15 (SLG Press, 2nd edn, 2000).

——, *The Face of Love: Meditations on the Way of the Cross* (SLG Press, 1977).

Sister Susan SLG, *Our Deepest Desire: Prayer, Fasting and Almsgiving in the Teaching of Augustine of Hippo*, Fairacres Publications 193 (SLG Press, 2022).

St Teresa of Avila, *The Collected Works of St. Teresa of Avila*, vol. 1: *The Book of Her Life, Spiritual Testimonies, Soliloquies*, trans. by Kieran Kavanaugh and Otilio Rodriguez (ICS Publications, 2nd rev. edn 1987).

William Roscoe Thayer, *Life and Letters of John Hay* (1915).

R. S. Thomas, 'But the Silence in the Mind' (1990), published in *Collected Later Poems 1998–2000: Counterpoint*, part 4, 'AD' (Bloodaxe Books, 2004).

Jean Vanier, *Community and Growth* (Paulist Press, 1989).

Sr Benedicta Ward SLG, ed., *The Desert of the Heart: Daily Readings with the Desert Fathers*, introd. and ed. Sr Benedicta Ward SLG (SLG Press, 2016, 2nd edn 2022).

——, *The Wisdom of the Desert Fathers: Systematic Sayings from the Anonymous Series of the* Apophthegmata Patrum (SLG Press, 2011).

Raymond Wells, *Leo Buscaglia – In His Own Words* (Amazon Digital Services, 2021).

Macrina Wiederkehr, *A Tree Full of Angels: Seeing the Holy in the Ordinary* (HarperSanFrancisco, 1990).

Rowan Williams, *Where God Happens: Discovering Christ in One Another* (Shambhala, 2007).

Valentine Zander, *Saint Seraphim of Sarov: His Life* (Fellowship of St Alban & St Sergius, 1968).

SLG PRESS PUBLICATIONS

slgpress.co.uk